The
Ron Sanderson
Collection

A selection of photographs
taken in Sheffield 1960s - 1980s

©A. Colgrave, J. Colgrave September 2005
www.ronsandersoncollection.com

Printed and published by:
ALD Design & Print
279 Sharrow Vale Road
Sheffield S11 8ZF

Telephone 0114 267 9402
E:mail a.lofthouse@btinternet.com

ISBN 1-901587-57-6

First published: October 2005

Ronald Lester Sanderson
1944 - 1994

Ron Sanderson was born in the Park district of Sheffield in January 1944. He grew up on Skye Edge Road with his parents Lily and George and two sisters, Pat and Janet.

He attended Manor Lodge Primary and First School and went on to Hurlfield Comprehensive. In 1959 he won a scholarship to Sheffield College of Arts and Crafts. Ron joined his Father in the steel works as a smither but still attended college in the evenings. He was a talented artist and became an avid photographer.

Ron photographed many parts of his beloved city and people - he would walk many miles taking pictures of ordinary people and their everyday lives.

In the mid Seventies he achieved one of his ambitions - to have his photographs displayed in the city's Graves Art Gallery. This (a one man exhibition)led to his work being shown all over the country.

He continued to photograph Sheffield's changes throughout the Seventies and Eighties. In the early 1990s, he sadly became ill with cancer and following a long fight with this, he died in 1994.

Ron's memory will live on through his beautiful photographs.

    M. Sanderson

Ron Sanderson 31/1/44-08/05/94

Cityscapes   1

Abstract   13

Decay   23

People   33

Buildings   43

Workers   65

People & Places   73

Photograph details   77

Cityscapes

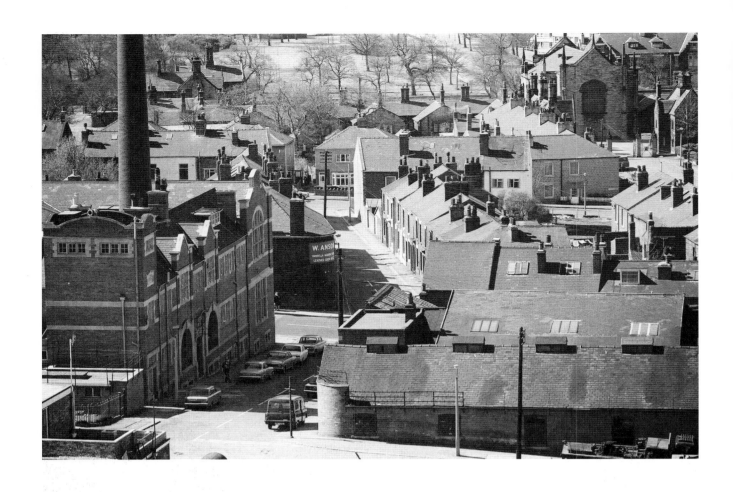

Abstract

15

Decay

25

People

40

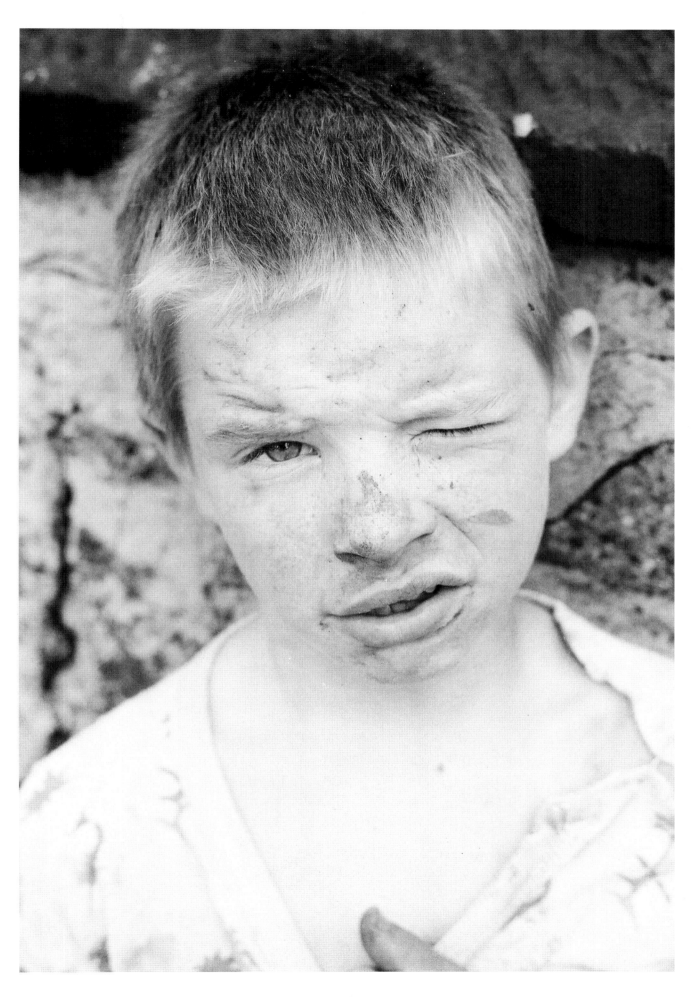

Buildings

45

49

61

Workers

People & Places

Photograph Details

1)   Park Hill flats from Sky Edge

2)   Maltravers Road in foreground with Cricket Inn Road behind

3)   Top: Park Hill and City Centre taken from maisonettes on Bernard Road
        Bottom: Victoria Quays and Durham Ox pub taken from hill at Broad
        Street

4)   Park Square roundabout under construction, Victoria Quays and
        Blast Street.

5)   Top: Hyde Park Flats & St. John's Church
        Bottom: Train station & City

6)   Top: Looking towards Duke Street and Norfolk Park
        Bottom: City Centre from behind Bernard Street Maisonettes
        (known as The Tiers)

7)   Before The Crucible was built view across to St. Marie's, Sheffield
        Catholic Cathedral with The Fiesta Club under construction in
        foreground.

8)   Top: Maisonettes in front of Hyde Park Flats
        Bottom: Fiesta club, Town Hall clock tower behind

9)   City Centre and bus station, complete with 'bendy bus'

10)   Looking towards Highfields from Heeley

11)   Top:
        Bottom: Broad Street towards Park Square roundabout

12)   Hyde Park Flats with gravestone pathway

13)   Hyde Park Steps

14)   Footbridge heading towards Victoria Quays

15)

16)   Pond Hill leading down from Fitzalan Square

17)   Blonk Street towards what is now the Bristol Hotel, then offices

18)   Whiteley Woods Clinic steps

19)   Trees at Hyde Park flats

20)   Boat hull mould at Victoria Quays

21)   Ladies bridge, joining of River Sheaf & River Don

22)

23)   Demolition of Sheffield's Rag & Tag market

24)   Demolition of Sheffield's Rag & Tag market

25)   Top: Sky Edge
        Bottom: Sheaf Market

26)   Top:
        Bottom: Shalesmoor, the famous Sheffield silversmithing company
        James Dixon located at Cornish place in background(closed 1990)

27)   Demolition around Duke Street

28)   The Lowdrop pub, Attercliffe

29)   Norfolk Arms on Gower Street

30)   Close up demolition on Duke Street

31)   Demolition of Firth Brown's, Brightside Lane

35)   An artist at work!

38)   Top: Norfolk Park

39)   Manor Oaks Road, off Duke Street

40)   Top: Norfolk Park

43)   Barkers Pool and Gaumont Cinema. This view taken in 1985 just
        before demolition of the Gaumont. It is also the latest
        photograph in this collection

44)   Top: Leadmill Road near the junction of St. Mary's Road
        Bottom: Myrtle Road off Queens Road, now the site of Halfords

45)   Victoria Quays

46)   Top: Duke Street
        Bottom: Montgomery pub, St Mary's Road. Building had lost its
        Top floor during the 1940 Blitz

47)   Commercial Street

48)   Commercial Street

49)   Top: Surrey Street
        Bottom: Kenning Building on Brown Street

50)   Top: Top of Church Street
        Bottom: Leopold Street

51)   Lyceum during one of its periods of closure

52)   Top: Side of Lyceum and Tudor Place
        Bottom: City library, Tudor Square and Surrey Street

53)   Top: Fitzalan Square
        Bottom: Sheaf Street

54)   Dixon Lane

55) Top: Victoria Quays

56) Gibralter Street and Furnace Hill

57) Blonk Street towards Lady's Bridge

58) Lady's Bridge, River Sheaf

59) Top: Pitsmoor, Ellesmere Road and top of Gower Street
     Bottom: Spital Hill

60) Top: Rear of Aizlewood's Mill
     Bottom: Nursery Street with derelict Aizlewood's Mill

61) Top: Queens Road
     Bottom: Stainforth Road

62) Brick-a-Brack shop, Heeley

63) Hill Top Chapel, Attercliffe, built 1637 and the resting place of
     Benjamin Huntsman

67) A R Heathcote, Fud Wright, George Sanderson (relative of Author)

69) Bottom: Working on the Inner Ring Road, St. Mary's Gate

73) Whiteley Wood Clinic

74) Top: Pigeon watchers, Sky Edge
     Bottom: Hyde Park, behind the Tiers

75) Top: Hyde Park Flats viewed from Pond Street
     Bottom: Rag & Tag Market

76) Ramp, The Tiers, Hyde Park

For photographs with no description we either do not know the location or, in the case of people, do
not know their names. Please let us know if you can identify any of these!

All these pictures and more are available to purchase
as prints from: www.ronsandersoncollection.com